T0128939

INSPIRE A HIRE

SUCCESSFUL JOB-HUNTING
STRATEGIES FOR EVERYONE

RICHARD HOBBS, BSc, FMM

iUniverse, Inc.
Bloomington

INSPIRE A HIRE
SUCCESSFUL JOB-HUNTING STRATEGIES FOR EVERYONE

iUniverse books may be ordered through booksellers or by contacting:

iUniverse
1663 Liberty Drive
Bloomington, IN 47403
www.iuniverse.com
1-800-Authors (1-800-288-4677)

Because of the dynamic nature of the Internet, any web addresses or links contained in this book may have changed since publication and may no longer be valid. The views expressed in this work are solely those of the author and do not necessarily reflect the views of the publisher, and the publisher hereby disclaims any responsibility for them.

Any people depicted in stock imagery provided by Thinkstock are models, and such images are being used for illustrative purposes only.

Certain stock imagery © Thinkstock.

ISBN: 978-1-4759-7889-6 (sc)
ISBN: 978-1-4759-7891-9 (e)

Library of Congress Control Number: 2013904054

Printed in the United States of America

iUniverse rev. date: 3/26/2013

"Having been made bankrupt as an entrepreneur, I had never written a CV or been for an interview in twenty-five years. Richard and this book helped restore my self-confidence as we worked together on my CV, and I won the interview I wanted within twenty-four hours of submitting my details. His coaching support on interview preparation and his help in creating a sales pitch presentation beat another candidate with more experience. I am extremely grateful to Richard for writing *Inspire a Hire* and helping me get back on track and will continue to use his skills in the future as I believe he has a real gift with this process from his experience."

Russell Kendall
Bankrupt Business Owner, UK

"Rich, you're amazing; your book and coaching helped me transform my CV. I got four interviews in one week and now have two jobs from it. You helped me realise how many skills I have and gave me the courage and confidence to be proactive and go for what I wanted."

Alison Jones
Student, UK

"Dear Rich, I was so lacking confidence after not having an interview for fifteen years and had no idea what to do. Your book made it easy for me to see the way forward and your supportive coaching prior to the interview helped me believe in myself and face the challenge. Thank you so much for your help."

Ian Geary
UK

Disclaimer

Whilst everything outlined and the examples given in this e-book, *Inspire a Hire,* have proved successful for me and others, it must be recognised that the recruiting process is highly competitive and the success of the interview process can often simply come down to non-verbal chemistry between an individual and the hiring manager. Therefore, this book guarantees neither interviews nor, ultimately, a job offer. The personal details on the winning CV examples in the appendices have been modified to protect the privacy of the clients.

They say that behind every great man is a great woman. Whilst I make no claims to greatness, I have survived a battle that millions lose thanks to my beautiful wife, Debbie, who has always believed in me through challenging times, and to Bethany, for showing me the greatest lesson of success. I love you both.

To my creator for the blessings throughout my life and the gift placed in me of helping others.

'Persistence and Determination are Omnipotent'

CONTENTS

ABOUT *INSPIRE A HIRE*

If you are a young or long-term job hunter, someone who has been made redundant after many years of service with one company, a housewife or -husband returning to work, or even the career professional who is on the move, then this book will take you directly to lessons that get results.

Ask yourself, 'Would I benefit right now from any of the following?'

- Actual examples of successful interview-winning CVs

- Knowledge of how to pass a recruiter's ten-second visual test

- Pre-, during, and post-interview lessons from successful job hunters

- A technique for inspiring the hiring manager with STAR answers

- The truth about the recruitment process

- How to stay employed in a competitive market

If you answered yes to any of the above then, this book is definitely what you need right now. My goal for *Inspire a Hire* is to provide a simple and effective tool that will help job hunters generate interviews and ultimately achieve their desired careers.

In my twenty years' business experience, some of which were spent as a recruitment consultant reviewing CVs and working with hiring managers, I have successfully beaten the competition for employment within an often depressed marketplace. I have helped many clients do so as well.

Having been through many changes in my career due to redundancy and my drive to succeed, I have experienced hundreds of interviews and invested time and money working alongside job coaches. This has enabled me to develop genuine job-hunting skills and to assist other job hunters.

The following pages present the essence of my experience from my job-seeking journey and from coaching others in the job-hunting process. This is not a self-development book or a get-rich-quick text but a tool to prevent you from wasting your time and money on products and services that lack my authentic, heart-driven intent.

In the following pages, I will guide you to a winning structure that has, in my job-hunting journey, cost me several hundred pounds to discover and gone through many iterations since I first wrote it down. My goal is to accelerate your learning and take you straight to the best solutions, as any good mentor would do. Teaching you the lessons my clients and I have learned through difficult experience.

This book is about the truth of the recruitment industry, about the essential requirements for making a visual impact with your CV, in a world driven by perceptions. It is about simple lessons learned from years of career dissatisfaction and change. It is about gaining clarity on what success really means for you, to help you avoid missing the roses on the way.

The Internet is full of free material on CV writing and interview techniques. Free information may give you quick answers, but the methodology presented here, developed from hours of research and consultations with CV experts, provides you with a holistic approach to job hunting and career success.

Somewhere along the road, I believe businesses' passion for serving the customer has been lost in their desire for profit. Some CV-writing companies will recommend changes to your CV simply to generate a sale. A relatively easy method of beating the competition has become overcomplicated with rules and beliefs, such as the two-page rule, that simply, in my experience, create an illusion for the job hunter.

My aim is to provide you with an easy and quick guide, without all the waffle, to standing out from the herd and getting what you want.

It is my hope that *Inspire a Hire* will help millions of job hunters across the world. The cost of this e-book is a small investment for the knowledge that has helped others develop confidence and see themselves as added value in the marketplace. Ask yourself right now:

What would I be willing to invest to get the job of my dreams?

1 INTRODUCTION

A Welcome and Words of Encouragement

Dear Job Hunter,

Welcome to *Inspire a Hire*.

You are already a success because you are here for a positive reason!

You might be here because:

- You're serious about securing the job, career, and lifestyle you want.

- You're looking for your first job or have been employed in the same company for many years and face redundancy, thinking you would never need to write a CV or embark on job hunting. The truth is, the job market can be a minefield.

- You're not be getting past the recruitment systems that send you those disheartening letters that say, 'Regrettably, on this occasion you have been unsuccessful', with no feedback to help you identify how to improve.

- You're proactive and not a quitter. My guess is you're also determined to get what you want!

So congratulations!

You're already ahead of the majority of job hunters who randomly fire off a poorly drafted CV into the electronic ether and wonder why they don't receive any calls. Whatever your reason for being here now, I want to welcome you to this practical, tested approach to getting interviews and, ultimately, offers for the job you desire.

My mission in the following pages is to teach you the proven approach that has helped me, and others, move jobs and significantly increase earnings relatively quickly, even during an economic recession and in a highly competitive market.

The lessons presented here, if you choose to apply them, will help your CV pass a recruiter's ten-second-scan test, will emphasise your added value, and will make you someone to take seriously as a potential candidate.

I am going to help you realise what your unique selling point is – and yes, you are unique. There is no other being like you in the universe. So know your uniqueness; it will make you stand out from the crowd. A great thing to know at the start of this e-book journey is that these are simple lessons learned from experience that require only a little logic and creativity to apply.

All I ask is for you to trust what I have learned from my own job-hunting experience and from other job hunters. Apply it, and then let me know your result by emailing your success story to me at mycoach@inspireahire.com.

I believe that you have what it takes to add value to any organisation because as Stephen Covey tells us the first habit of highly successful people is to *be proactive*. So read on, my friend, and let us travel together towards the success you desire.

May you be blessed with achieving your unique vision of success, whatever that vision may be.

Well done!

Rich Hobbs, BSc, FMM
Your Job-Hunting Coach

2 THE RECRUITMENT REALITY

An Experiential Insight into the Recruitment Industry

So, you have spent time searching for the job or career that turns a light on inside you, and you're confident that latest application and CV will be a winner. You prepare a CV to the best of your ability and hit the Send button, or maybe even lick a stamp the good, old-fashioned way, and say quietly to yourself, 'Please, God, let this be the one.'

Whatever the method required for the application, you have actually made progress, and you're hopeful of a positive result. The days go by, then a couple of weeks, and still you have not heard anything. You go over your application, wondering why you haven't received a response, and you eventually muster the courage to ring up the agency or employer, only to hear the classic phrase:

'Unfortunately, your details did not match our requirements. We will keep your details on file.'

Hanging up the phone, your stomach sinks with the disappointment of rejection. Then begin the self-analysis and internal chatter that may negatively impact your emotional state. Those nearest to you see you're upset, and you have to announce that you did not even get an interview.

Does this sound familiar?

Believe me, I know this very well, and I've spent several years doing what can only be madness, as we have been told that 'to do the same thing repeatedly expecting a different result'. Until I learned the lessons I will be outlining in the following pages about the reality of the recruitment process.

Sales Drive Behaviour

According to the classic book *The Goal* by E. Goldratt, the reason most organisations exist is pure and simple: to make a profit! This is their sole purpose – they do nothing more and nothing less. All behaviour within these organisations is driven by sales and profit margins to achieve this goal.

So let's enter the mind of the recruitment consultant. Having been a recruitment consultant for a couple of years, I have a sound insight into this role and know that having this reality check should increase your chances for success.

Imagine that your job security is strongly dependent on achieving sales for the agency and hitting your targets, and success means placing candidates into jobs. That's also how you achieve your bonus.

How focused would you be?

How much time would you be willing to give candidates who do not make a serious attempt to communicate their work experience clearly?

What is the underlying goal in the back of the recruiter's mind?

Reflect on this for a moment.

The Process

At some point, an employer loses a member of staff, decides to expand the team, or even creates a brand new role. This is the birth of opportunity for you as the job hunter. The employer will decide either to run their own recruitment campaign or utilise one of the many recruitment agencies. And so the process begins.

The recruitment agencies' clients who are hiring need to explain what they are looking for in the ideal candidate. This could be a brief conversation with the recruitment consultant, who scribbles down the job description, or a detailed face-to-face meeting where the client clearly knows what he or she needs and provides a detailed job specification, a candidate profile, and a list of both essential and desirable qualities for the position.

The recruitment consultant negotiates a fee with the client, which may be that the agency receives a percentage of the successful candidate's salary. This is the typical approach for permanent vacancies; however, a fixed charge may be applied. Whatever financial arrangements are made, the recruiter is hungry to win the business, as this industry is highly competitive. Once the recruiter has some sense of what the customer desires in a candidate, he or she will work an advertising campaign to attract that candidate.

In an ideal world, where time is in abundance, the above process would be done thoroughly, with the recruiter getting a clear understanding of the client's needs and job hunters getting full details of the job specifications. However, the recruiters and client are driven by pressure to find a new employee, and they go through this process so quickly that they often overlook details. The understanding of the client's need by the recruiter and the recruiter's objectives by the client is somewhat grey.

The next step in the process is the advert. Potential candidates will be attracted by the job title, salary, and other content it gives. They will prepare their covering letters and CVs and then apply for the role. The recruiter will review applications and match candidates' experience to the job specifications. In this selection process, the recruiter highlights some candidates as potentials and rejects the rest. The client is then presented with the selected potentials to review to decide whom to interview. This final filtering process is often performed by the hiring manager, who is also under pressure to fill the gap in his or her team.

Tip! Candidate filtering is now mostly done automatically by smart computer systems that look for keywords, so your CV's wording and spelling are critical!

This whole process depends on human interpretation of a workplace task, which ends up in the form of a job specification. This following point is what I want you to grasp:

Tip! The recruiter does not often really understand the actual job being offered. The company's HR team is unlikely to have performed the role being advertised, and the hiring manager is likely too busy to get hands-on experience of the role. Therefore, you need to recognise that this whole process is open to misinterpretation of the common characteristics or skills that someone needs to perform the role.

And here is the opportunity you must see:

Tip! You do not have to be an exact match to get through a recruiter's filtering system. I repeat, because it is very important: you do not have to be an exact match to the job specification.

Recruiters are there to prevent hiring managers from spending hours sifting through hundreds, sometimes thousands, of applications to find their new employee. Good candidates will get through the filters if they fully absorb and understand the detail of the job specification and emphasise their key characteristics that best fit those details in their covering letter and CV.

Tip! Do *not* be put off or disheartened by what you read in a job vacancy advert.

An open job vacancy is an opportunity waiting for your skills. However, I would not suggest applying for a neurosurgeon's role if you have no medical training, but I'm hoping this is quite obvious! Understand the key features of the role, grasp the advert's core content, see the needs of the employer, identify the experience and skills required, and review how your own experience and skills match those.

If the advert is poor, by this I mean very brief and non-specific, then move on to something else, as the hiring company do not really know what they want. Alternatively you could ring them and ask for a detailed job specification. If they cannot meet this request, then consider whether you really want to work for that company, as such a lack of communication and clear information is not the mark of a quality organisation.

The recruiter is under pressure to achieve sales and will not spend time review-ing a poorly written covering letter or CV. He or she will scan your application in ten to fifteen seconds. The recruiter will scan for keywords and key phrases denoting certain skills and experience that match his or her interpretation of what the customer needs. If the recruiter registers a match in his or her mind within these first ten to fifteen seconds, then he or she will invest more time in taking a closer look; otherwise, the recruiter will reject the application. This is the *ten-second-scan test*.

Therefore, you *must* ensure that you express in your covering letter how, spe-cifically, you are a good match to the company's needs. As stated, you don't have to meet all the criteria, but you must make it jump out that you are the best fit. Your CV must also clearly show keywords and key phrases indicating experience and skills to register as a hit in the mind of the recruiter. So, if you really want to get in front of the hiring manager, be prepared to make adjust-ments to your covering letter and CV for every application you make to design each application as a match.

> **Tip! One standard covering letter and CV do not fit all situations.**

Again, recruiters will not spend hours trying to work out what your skills really are and then go out and sell you to employers. The majority of a recruiter's job is to simply match his or her interpretation of a need.

If you tell them, specifically, how you are the best fit, you will make their job simple and stand out, because many people apply for jobs without considering what specifically the employer requires, and recruiters become swamped with wasteful activity.

When you take the time to specifically tailor your application documents to match the employers requirements, recruiters will see you as a potential sale and will make efforts to convince hiring employers that you are the candidate before a competitor beats them to the sale. You then become a marketable asset for the recruiting agency. If you help the recruiter by telling them clearly how you are a match, some agencies will actively approach clients and sell you into the organisation.

Hiring managers will follow the same logic. Their minds will register keyword matches to skills and other criteria. When you do eventually get in front of them, they may overlook many of the specification requirements and instead consider them as areas for training. Thus, the job specifications become simply a guide, not the deciding factor for hiring.

Once your application has been approved and you've had an interview, many managers will ask themselves the following questions in assessing whether to give you the job.

- Do I feel comfortable with this candidate?

- Could I work with this person?

- Can this person be trained?

- Do I like this person's attitude?

Interviewing, which is intended to be a fair process based on well-defined criteria, simply boils down to non-verbal signals and your ability to create a relationship within a short meeting. This will be covered later, in a discussion on the actual interview.

Remember! You do not have to be an exact match, so relax.

I deeply want you to know the nature of the animal you are dealing with so you can tame it and make it your servant to get you the interviews you deserve and thus achieve your dream.

Let us look now at the CV structure that has proven successful for many job hunters.

3 · A WINNING STRUCTURE

A Step-by-Step Structure of Some Successful CVs

So there you have it, a personal insight into the reality of the recruitment process that you are dealing with and some valuable guidance on what steps to take to pass the ten-second-scan test. Now let's get into the detail of the design of the vehicle that will increase your chances of winning the interview. Keep this famous quote in mind throughout the process:

> Everything should be made as simple
> as possible, but not simpler.
> —*Albert Einstein*

Within the world of professional CV writing, there is no one standard format for this document, but some common themes and styles have emerged over time.

What follows is a simple-to-follow method that has proven to be successful and will guide you step by step to creating an interview-winning CV. If you like to jump straight to the answers page, then check out the appendices and study the examples of actual interview- and job-winning CVs.

It is worth noting that there are different types of CVs, including chronological, functional, and combined. Most of this e-book is about a chronological CV, but if you want to learn more about the other types, check out appendix D now. But make sure you come right back!

Welcome back. You did have a look, didn't you?

The structure you need to use will depend on how you want to present yourself. As I have said before, be prepared to create a new version for each unique opportunity if you want to be an interview winner. Keep this thought in the back of your mind:

Important! One size does not fit all.

Real job-winning example CVs appear in the appendices of this book to illustrate the finished CVs I have written for clients who were successful on the job hunt, and a couple of great testimonials from a young job seeker and a bankrupt business owner also appear.

My objective is to walk you through the building blocks of a winning format and to show you examples to reference when creating your own unique, winning CV.

Here is the structure I have found to be highly successful. But remember – there is no definitive standard:

1. Your name and contact details. This may seem obvious, but many people fail here.

2. Your personal profile (the sales pitch). This is often very weak.

3. Career highlights (three to four key results/savings/awards).

4. Career history. This is what hiring managers really use to match you against the job specification, your actual experience.

5. Training/education. Remember, this is also about personality.

6. Key skills (three to four skills you are confident to discuss)

You can include hobbies, interests, and references, but I have learned that these things are rarely the primary focus for the recruiter or hiring manager. Writing standard comments like 'I enjoy reading and socialising' add virtually zero value to your CV. However, some hobbies and interests may have desirable qualities (e.g., youth leader, sports coach, running an online business). So expand your thinking and add an interest if you believe it contains an added-value skill set.

References are good to include if you have them and have informed them that they will be contacted. Most employers now send emails directly to the referee requesting reference details. Often, employers will not contact referees, as the process often only confirms that you were actually employed where you say you were and is an added cost to the hiring organisation.

At this point, if you are only starting out in your working life, you may have a sinking feeling that you have no career highlights or key skills to list. If you feel this way, please go straight to appendix F and see Alison Jones's winning CV. This young job hunter thought she had no skills until she received a little coaching.

Your Profile, the Unique You!

The first section of your CV – contact details – is not something I need to explain, but it is worth noting that you must get someone to check this for you because the last thing you want is an error in your contact details that leaves you un-contactable. Hyperlink your email address and test that the link works, as this helps the recruiter to email you quickly. Avoid writing 'Curriculum Vitae' at the top of your CV, as it is self-explanatory.

Now, let us look closely at your profile – the hook that will catch prospective employers' attention.

If you have seen *The Apprentice* with Sir Alan Sugar on TV, you know that the whole process is about sales ability. Fail to sell and you're fired! Get your pitch right, make a profit, and you're headed for the job. In the final, the candidates have to understand marketing, develop a brand image, be unique, and sell their product to achieve the business goal of making a profit.

This is the purpose of your profile. It is an opening advertisement that hooks the reader into your story. It is here that you have an opportunity to display your unique selling point, to say briefly what the sum of your experience is and what specifically you are looking for next. Here, you show that you are what the recruiter is looking for, and before the recruiter reads on, his or her sub-conscious has already registered a match to the job. Get your pitch right, and the reader will want to know more. 'What do I write about myself?' I hear you thinking. This may seem a challenge, but it only requires a little bit of creativity, logic, and self-confidence.

Ask yourself the following questions:

- What do I feel is unique about me?

- What am I specifically experienced at?

- How many years of experience do I have?

- What industry do I have experience in?

- What career level do I want to aim for?

- What is my highest qualification?

- What is my aspiration?

- What do I really want next in my career?

- Do I have specific or uncommon experience?

- What do I have that will add value to my new employer?

I could go on and on, so I will stop and allow you to think about those while I present the following examples to stimulate your creativity. What I would strongly recommend *not* to do is write a few lines that go something like this:

A very motivated worker with a positive attitude, good timekeeping, and a track record of good attendance.

'Why not?' you ask. Because this is for job hunters who do not really want to inspire a hire, as these qualities are expected of any employee. They say very little about whom you really are, your aspirations, or your sense of direction.

The following should get you thinking:

Profile Example 1: Seventeen-Year-Old Student Alison Jones

Personal Profile

A focused individual who achieves and exceeds goals, as demonstrated at Hawsworth Community College, where I was awarded Hawsworth Hero. Currently looking for a full-time job where I can add value with my knowledge and skills, develop my capabilities for the future, gain new experiences after finishing my education.

Over the past year, I have expressed my creativity and determination in many different ways, including photography, fashion, and hiking. I have worked independently with an entrepreneurial spirit, successfully running a small online business selling vintage clothing. My excellent skills in ICT have enabled me to set up my business by researching the market and by creating financial spreadsheets of sales, a page to sell my items, and a logo. Taking pride in this small business, I have achieved 100% positive feedback from buyers. My long-term career goal is to be a teacher and to provide a service to people in some positive way.

The previous example tells us that this young job hunter is an achiever and has been recognised with an award. She states clearly what she is looking for and what her aspirations are. Interestingly enough, when I worked with this client, she thought she had no skills, but as I asked her questions, I discovered she is a young entrepreneur running an online business who clearly understands customer service. The profile demonstrates that she is proactive and takes pride in what she does. She is a doer who knows what she wants. I learned that she went on to win four jobs in two days after we worked together. Below is her letter to me:

> Rich, your support and coaching helped me transform my CV. I got four interviews in one week and now have two jobs from it. You helped me realise how many skills I have and gave me the courage and confidence to be proactive and go for what I wanted.
>
> Alison Jones – Student, UK

It was extremely rewarding to receive her note, especially at a time when many young job seekers are struggling to find opportunities. However, a lot needs to be said for the enthusiasm and effort Alison put into the process which, ultimately, is what makes the difference. You can view her interview-busting CV in appendix A.

Let us now consider another example from another client. Please feel free to jump to appendix A to view this client's complete CV, which has won him many interviews.

Profile Example 2: Experienced Professional

Quality Profile

A highly qualified quality professional with more than fifteen years' experience from quality technician to quality manager. The foundation of this professional's career is with the high-precision/high-quality British aerospace arena, gaining management experience with Massey Ferguson and then winning the prestigious Fellowship of Manufacturing Management Award as a change agent with Cranfield University. Moving then into the automotive market for MG Rover, he focused on problem resolution and preventative containment action.

> Studying part-time, this enthusiastic professional gained an ONC/ HNC and BSc in manufacturing with a primary focus in quality and quality systems. As a result of the combined experiential training and knowledge acquisition, this individual has a hands-on approach to personnel management and provides a supportive environment for improvement through knowledge sharing, synergy creation, and individual development. A positive envoy of change, he minimises resistance through the use of effective communication skills, working with colleagues to build open, honest, and productive relationships. *Now, at forty, this experienced professional within GE wants to hone his leadership experience in a first-time Quality Director role.*

Some recruiters and CV writing companies would say the above profile is too long. However, I have worked with this client over the past few years and know that he had many hits with this CV and went on to increase his earnings by twenty thousand pounds in the same period.

Remember! There is *no* absolute CV standard.

This profile immediately shows this candidate's experience and work history and shows a clear progression from technician into management. It shows a unique selling point by mentioning the Fellowship of Manufacturing Management scheme with Cranfield, a prestigious organisation. It refers to the candidate's education and characteristics as a leader. Finally, it clearly explains where the candidate is in his career and what his desired next step is: a first-time director role.

The previous two examples should give you some idea of what to create in your unique profile, and the suggested questions give you some food for thought. Now it's over to you to use some creativity. Before you start, a word of warning: avoid being so creative that you stray from the truth, as you may well be questioned on what you state here in your profile. Trust me – I know. I had a tough question once where I was asked to expand on my ability to create synergistic solutions to conflict, which I wrote in my profile, but stumbled in answering it.

May I Highlight My Successes?

Employers, as I am sure you are aware, do not pay employees to sit around all day drinking coffee and surfing the Net. They recruit people to assist the organisation in making a profit. Therefore, people who can demonstrate an ability to impact the bottom line with tangible savings are highly desirable.

Using a career highlights section at the beginning of your CV should immediately tell the hiring manager that you are likely to add value and provide improvements and, ultimately, cost savings to the organisation. In fact, I always recommend to clients that, each year, they should aim for adding tangible results to their CVs to promote career growth. The famous quality guru Tom Peters advocates in his book, *In Search of Excellence,* that if you are not able to add results to your CV, then you should reconsider what you are actually doing in your job.

Taken from the winning CV in appendix A, we see in the next example three specific results with tangible savings. The third point could be enhanced with the addition of financial savings or improvements in response times to customers.

Quality Career Highlights

- Generated savings of £1 million for Massey as a result of developing an expert understanding of the warehouse management system and eliminating unnecessary inspection.

- Served as project manager of a systems project to deliver a bolt-on to SAP solution for the handling of non-conformance materials, resulting in £100,000 savings for Caterpillar.

- Designed and developed a database for complaints management and improved the departmental corrective-action processes.

To generate your highlights, reflect on your career and write down everything you can remember, and keep this list close at hand as it will serve you in your interview. I once even contacted a previous employer to find out how much was actually saved financially as a result of a task I performed. Once you have three to four examples, you can use them as your STAR achievement stories, something we will cover in chapter 5. However, if you want to look ahead to the STAR principle, jump to appendix C, but promise to come straight back to this section!

Here you have another guiding principle for your winning CV: reflect on and identify your successes and achievements. Then, to stand out from the competition, select three to four key examples to emphasise in your CV highlights section to the recruiter as another selling point.

I can hear your inner voice whispering to you, 'But have I not achieved anything. I have no real successes.' This is a common reaction, as most people do not recognise their successes or achievements. So just ask yourself: What have I done that may be relevant? Then allow a couple of days to ponder this and see what your amazing subconscious mind reminds you of. Once you have the answer, capture it in your highlights section. Go for it! You can do it!

What Roles Have You Been Playing? – The Body of Your CV

We have discussed the profile and highlights for your CV, which grab attention quickly. Now, we will consider the roles you have played in either paid or unpaid work to build the main body of your interview-winning CV. This section is focused on getting factual statements onto paper –clear bullet points about your key responsibilities and the types of tasks you performed. In a nutshell, you'll write what it was you did during each period of your working life.

Accomplishing this requires acknowledging basic principles shown in the appendices and an understanding of the recruiter's mindset. The recruiter is primarily interested in matching your previous experience to his or her vacancy to establish a quick win, a sale. So think carefully about what job titles you use and, if necessary, do a little research if you need to adjust your titles to match industry-standard roles.

I am not suggesting that you say you have performed a role you have not. Instead, you should avoid glamorous and overly creative titles that are not commonly used in your industry, as these may prevent you from being matched by automatic search engines and electronic filtering systems.

The current technology used by the recruitment business searches for keywords or key phrases in your CV to accelerate the matching process. The recruiter's mind works in exactly the same manner, searching for certain keywords. So, understand your market's language and use it to your advantage.

The recruiter or employer will scan your CV from left to right, as is common when reading documents, so placing your job title first, then the company name, then the period of employment helps the recruiter quickly scan the left side of your CV to absorb the types of roles you have performed.

Below is an extract from appendix A that demonstrates the recommended layout of your employment experience:

Quality Manager   Quantum Elastomers (Aerospace) (March 2010 to June 2010)

- Handled all customer complaint resolution.

- Conducted internal audit.

- Managed the inspection team (two people).

- Upheld company approvals.

- Managed despatch/trim/inspection (three people).

In this example, we can clearly see the what, who, and when for this candidate's role. We see *what* the role was in bold, *who* the previous employer was, and *when* this candidate worked there. Your CV's employment history section requires nothing more than these basic facts, which the recruiter will be looking for.

Once the recruiter or employer has a feel for the roles you have played, he or she will, if a match is sensed, look more closely at the specific bullet points you have written. This information enhances the recruiter's ability to match your skills to the detail of the client's job specification. Tailoring your language in this section to match the job specification is essential to achieving a win.

As the industry standard has evolved to suggest keeping this document to two pages at the maximum, the number of lines you display is restricted. However, it is my experience that now being in the electronic era, a CV that extends to three or even four pages will not be rejected for professionals with a lengthy period of service.

However, stick to the principle of 'less is more' and, whatever you do, avoid writing long paragraphs instead of brief bullets about roles and responsibilities wherever possible.

Critical Success Factor! If it is not clear and easy to read, your CV is likely to be directed to the reject pile.

As shown in the above example, the objective is to write a brief line or two that tell the reader exactly what you did – nothing more, nothing less. Think in terms of facts that match you to the job specification. Once you have captured all the key points you would like to share, then move on to you next position.

Note: list your most recent employment first.

Tip! For people like me who have had several roles over a long period, it is not necessary to detail every job you have performed, as the last five years are typically the main area of interest. When this is the case, show the last three roles in detail, and then, for the remain-

der, simply state the job title, company, and period of employment.

If the employer wants to know more, he or she will ask you to talk about these roles during the interview.

Another important point to note here is that you may want to emphasise a specific period of experience in your career most relevant to the role you are applying for. In this case, it is helpful to the recruiter if you prepare a functional CV, which emphasises the specific work experience that matches the job vacancy's requirements, rather than a chronological CV.

I have used the functional CV approach several times. Recently, I coached an entrepreneur who was forced to close his business as a result of economic conditions and whose goal was to gain employment as a short-term solution. He had never, in twenty years, even considered writing a CV! We wrote a functional CV, matching his relevant experience to his desired role, and he won an interview within twenty-four hours of applying. With further coaching, he went on to win the position. The following letter is his very rewarding feedback to me:

> Dear Rich,
>
> I wish to sincerely thank you for all your support and coaching over the last month. Having been a self-employed director of my own company, which has been forced to close due to economic conditions, I really believed that I had no real prospects of obtaining a new career.
>
> I had not written a CV for nearly twenty years and had never needed to find employment.
>
> With your constructive guidance in writing a CV, I applied for a sales executive job, learning from you that the CV was a critical part of winning the interview. Your knowledge of the present working climate and understanding of the selection process helped ensure I got an interview.
>
> With your further coaching on interview techniques, I managed to

progress to the final two at second interview stage and was asked to prepare a PowerPoint presentation. Having never used this medium before, this was an immediate challenge. Thankfully, with your help and expertise, we created a unique presentation that fulfilled all the objectives asked of me.

The second interview was three hours in duration and was quite gruelling, but with your guidance and instruction, I attended with the self-assurance to present both professionally and with real confidence.

Your post-interview follow-up advice of emailing a small thank-you to the key person I interviewed with helped me to look professional and efficient.

The other candidate, who was to be interviewed two days later, had more relevant, proactive experience and a track record in sales of the specific product. I was not, therefore, expecting to get any further in the face of such competition. However, I was immensely pleased with all I had learned from you, the self-belief it had instilled in me and the experience of the interview. It gave me the self-belief to apply for further positions and step out into the current employment market.

On the Friday of the same week as my interview, I had a call from the company's HR department. I believed that I was receiving a courtesy call to advise me I had been unsuccessful. However, to my shock and surprise, I *did* get the position! I was commended on the time and effort I had put into the preparation for the position and with your professional input, I had secured a job that I didn't think I would ever get.

I write this with real gratitude for your time, experience and expertise, which has guided me to getting a position that will enhance my future. I would recommend your services to anyone needing to progress in their career or have a change in circumstances. Your services provided the opportunity to get a foot in the door, to stand out from the majority with a professional CV, and assistance on interview and presentation techniques.

Many thanks once again, Rich.

Kind regards,
Russell Kendall

I always see such encouraging feedback as a blessing that fills me with enormous gratitude that I can be of service to job hunters.

Let us now get back to our mission.

The race is nearly at an end, and you will have reached an important milestone in your winning CV creation if you have followed my recommendation. You have, haven't you? Of course you have! Your being here right now shows how proactive you are, having got this far! Congratulations. We are almost ready to get you on the market. Please read on.

What Qualifies You to Be Here?

Many people often do not hold high opinions of the well-qualified or academically enlightened, and they state that they have been trained by the 'university of life'. This is a perfectly acceptable viewpoint, as life teaches us rich lessons from experience that we simply cannot learn within the covers of a book. However, in business, the reality is that organisations use your education and training to gauge your understanding of a specific body of knowledge required to perform a role.

The qualifications area of your CV lists your training and qualifications. The preferred layout can be found in the appendices to clearly show you the result you need to achieve.

Quality Training & Qualifications

1994 BSc in Industrial (Quality) Systems Technology
1991 HNC in Production Engineering
1989 ONC in Mechanical and Production Engineering
2006 Internal QMS ISO9001 Auditor
2003 Six Sigma Green Belt
2007 A1 NVQ Assessor
2008 LRQA Lead Auditor ISO 9001:2000
1990 NVQ Level IV Quality Technician Engineer
2003 Targeted Selection Interviewer

1999 LEAN Trainer Training
1996 IMS Interpersonal Management Course

Tip! If the job specification clearly calls for specific qualifications, then list them first for absolute clarity to assist the recruiter matching your qualifications.

In the UK, National Vocational Qualifications (NVQs) are now a key factor recruiters consider in achieving standards of performance and service.

Those candidates who can list and provide objective evidence of qualifications hold greater chances of employment. I know a guy who is extremely gifted and highly intelligent but who has never been able to forge any sustainable career path owing to his lack of formal qualifications. So there it is: qualifications and training definitely support your winning CV. Whatever you have done that is relevant, make note of it in your CV.

Tip! If you decide to use a key skills section on your CV, ensure you make it rich with keywords specific to your industry sector to enable search engines to find you.

Work with the keys skill summary in appendix B to get the job done, and then check your document for typos.

Many recruiters will reject a CV with spelling mistakes, as in the twenty-first century, we have the wonderful spell-checking software, so please remember to use it.

Understand that having few or no qualifications will not instantly reject you from society and result in a life of suffering or limited income. The demand for qualifications is simply a reality of current business practice.

Achieving success requires an idea, a vision, and the determination and to believe in yourself and your goals, and persistence as you take action to achieve those goals. These success factors gave us the greatest of leaders and achievers in history. Success is whatever you define it to be. Many people believe, as I do, that genuine inner peace and contentment is the deepest desire of even the wealthiest people on the planet.

During my travels across India, I saw the most joyful and genuine of smiles amidst the worst poverty on the planet. The answer and conclusion to the definition of success is personal to you, my friend. So, I will leave that for you to decide. The deep subject of the spirituality of success is covered further in chapter 8, at the end of *Inspire a Hire*.

4 GETTING OUT THERE

Successful Approaches to Making You Visible

My goal in writing *Inspire a Hire* is to provide a simple and effective tool that will help job hunters generate interviews quickly and, ultimately, achieve their desired career opportunity. This chapter will point you towards techniques for online job hunting that many job hunters have found effective.

This area of discussion is a subject in its own right, if you want to expand further, I recommend a great book called *What Color Is Your Parachute?* This reference text has been revised year on year now for the last ten years. I have found it very useful on my journey, specifically with regard to mapping out what I really want from a job role.

Cyber CVs

It is my hope that what I have written so far has fostered in you an understanding and has inspired you to begin creating your unique CV, a marketing document that will generate interviews for you. Assuming you now have this document ready to launch into the marketplace, what exactly do you do with it?

Some view the use of electronically distributing your CV across the World Wide Web as not being the most effective strategy for gaining interviews. In some cases, the random distribution of your CV can be a total waste of time.

Fortunately, the fast-paced world of technology has moved on, and the experience of my clients and me is that the Internet is now the most widely used tool for job hunters. Employers worldwide now expect applicants to submit an electronic CV to one of the many job boards.

Wherever you are in the world right now, I recommend you identify the key recruiters or job sites in your country and start uploading your details.

What to Look for in an Internet Job Site

Thousands of job sites where you can post your details according to your industry sector are now available on the Internet. What I have found over the years is that many of these sites have poor search engines. The screens that are designed to help you find the specific job you are looking for do not provide any real detail to search on. The search results you get are many jobs that do not really match the criteria you entered, which becomes very frustrating.

The best search engine I have found in the UK is www.jobsite.co.uk, as it allows a wide range of search options and actually gives you the results you are looking for. It allows you to upload a profile of exactly what you want in a job for recruiters to view instantly. This site sets the standard of what to look for in an Internet job site. If a site doesn't meet its standards, you can waste lots of time getting few results. You will need to invest the time to properly upload your details onto a few sites, but once you've done that, you are then visible to the global community.

> **Tip! Record which sites you have uploaded your CV to and, at least once a month, reload your CV to the site, as many recruiters will search for recently uploaded CVs so they only find fresh job hunters. This helped me to keep the calls coming. Please *double check* your contact details before posting!**
>
> **Fact! The Internet is now a key source for employers to**

search for resources. They employ software that trawls through masses of data, searching for keywords and common language to identify potential candidates and automatically filter them. Know the language of your industry and use keywords to your advantage.

The Targeted Approach

If you stop and ask yourself what it is that you really want, you will focus your thinking and guide the job-hunting process. Randomly applying for anything and everything you see, aiming for quantity rather than quality, is likely to take a lot of effort and deliver a disappointing result. It might work for you, but I wouldn't recommend it.

Being clear on what you really want enables you to work towards the first goal of job hunting: to identify through research specific organisations that have the characteristics you know you need to get from an employer (e.g., location, flexitime, childcare, health care, market leader, product type). This targeted approach requires time for researching organisations and may not initially feel productive, like you are achieving your goal of finding work. The benefit, however, is that you are increasing your potential to find, or even create, the exact role you want.

Once you have identified your target companies, you can create a very specific letter of approach directed to each company's managing director or HR department telling them exactly why you are contacting the company, what your skills and qualities are, and how you want to add value to the organisation. It is very possible that your contact with the organisations' decision-makers may arrive at a time that your skills and qualities match an idea or objective of theirs, and they will want to have a discussion with you.

So, what is it that you really want? Any old job, a career, or a lifestyle?

How Wide Is Your Net?

Successful job hunters understand that achieving the result of a job is about knowing how to market yourself. The CV is the product specification that you offer potential employers (customers). The challenge, as in any business venture, is attracting and winning customers – the essence of sales and marketing.

Your net is your network of contacts and relationships that you can utilise in getting yourself out there. Networking is a life skill key to creating opportunities for yourself. The old saying 'It's not what you know but who you know' is often true for the job hunter.

I recommend you use all your email contacts, all your phone contacts, and friends, relatives, and previous co-workers. Tell people you meet in the pub or at a restaurant about your job search and what you are looking for. Make everyone you know aware that you are actively looking for work, share your CV so your contacts can forward it to others.

> **Fact! Network, network, network. This is essential for interview creation. People will not seek you if they do not know who or where you are or what you have to offer.**
>
> **Tip! Save the contact details of every recruiter you receive an email enquiry from after you have made yourself visible on the Internet. This will build your network. Do this exercise for the rest of your life so you can reach hundreds of people in seconds via email. Your network can be a powerful resource, so build it and maintain it.**

Effective job hunters are the ones who apply the above guidelines as a personal habit. These principles are the foundations for personal growth and opportunity creation. They are life skills that can support your deeper sense of security and fulfilment.

Newspapers and Journals

Traditional newspapers and professional journals are still being printed and sometimes offer opportunities, so do not discount them from your job search as part of your targeted approach. The larger professional institutions and newspapers typically now post vacancies online and tools for searching and browsing through them, so consider these in your strategy.

Social Media and LinkedIn

Now with social media tools like Facebook and LinkedIn, many people are networking and advertising jobs via this method. You can advertise yourself quite simply on LinkedIn and get people you have worked with to endorse your skills and experience. Recruiters are now actively advertising roles on LinkedIn, so it is wise to keep this tool close at hand. I recently read that one guy advertised his experience on Facebook and was successfully approached by a company and gained work.

Listen Very Closely; I Shall Say This Only Once

Listening carefully to what is going on around you is a very important skill to develop if you want to pursue opportunities. What I mean is that wherever you are during your waking hours, tune in to your environment and listen with one ear to what is being said around you.

As an example, you may well be having a meal in a restaurant and tune in to a conversation at the next table that suggests the speaker may be a business owner or a decision-maker. Politely introducing yourself at an appropriate time may well create an opportunity for you.

To close this chapter, I simply want to say to you, in summary, that the twenty-first century is quite clearly dominated by technology. Employers utilise technology for efficiency, so embrace it and make it work for you. Start building your network today and keep it growing to keep yourself out there.

We already know you are a proactive person, so use this strength, combined with the technological resources at your fingertips, to be your own sales and marketing guru.

Now go for it! I believe in you!

PRE-INTERVIEW PREPARATION

Essential Success Guidance for Serious Job Hunters

Well, you did it! You've studied this e-book, created your interview-winning CV, and marketed yourself. Well done! You have an interview for the job you have been seeking. So what can you do now to make yourself stand out from the other candidates (the herd)?

Preparing for an interview is easier than you think. It just requires a little research and some planning to help you stand out and present yourself with confidence.

So let's get started! Most organisations nowadays have websites. This makes identifying some key facts about your potential new employer a piece of cake. Companies that do not have websites or that provide only limited information on their sites are not serious players in today's business environment, so keep this in mind as you assess them, as much as they assess you.

Exercise

Take out a single blank A4 sheet of paper. We are going to draw a simple mind map. Draw a cloud or circle in the centre of the paper and write the company name in capital letters within it, plus the date and time of your interview. Also write down the names and job titles of the interviewers. 'Appendix E – A Mind Map Template' has been provided for you, so all you need to do print the template out and fill in the spaces provided. Start recording some facts about the organisation on the sheet, drawing additional clouds with lines from the centre.

The key facts to add to your map from the company's website are:

- Annual turnover (sales)
  This will help you understand the size of the organisation. Look to see if the website has a link to an annual report, which will indicate the organisation's performance. Has it seen growth over the past five years? Is it reporting profits? Has it acquired any other businesses or brands as part of expansion? Record on your mind map last year's turnover and any other points such as record profits, acquisition names, and expected forecast turnover.

- Product range
  Find and write down, in another cloud, the types of products or services they offer, as you may have first-hand experience of this market. Write down some unique details of the product or service, for example, 'specialist in unique software solutions to the manufacturing industry' or 'our systems are the only products on the market that deliver 100 L/sec'. Capture some specific detail, especially if you're interviewing for a technical role, as it could be a discussion point.

- Markets
  In which industry does the company operate (legal, aerospace, automotive, educational)? This will indicate the nature of the business. For example, I know from experience that automotive companies operate at a much faster and more demanding pace than those in the slower-moving aerospace market. These details may influence your desire to work for this organisation, as it has mine.

- Number of employees
  This is key to understanding the size of your potential employer and the likelihood of its having well-developed systems and procedures. However, you may well be specifically looking for a small family busi-

ness, where you are likely to gain a broader range of responsibilities. I'm confident you have already thought of this.

- CEO/other executives
Some companies post a message from the chief executive officer (CEO). Look for this and read it. Write down his or her name and any points of the message to remember during the interview.

  I have opened an interview with a discussion about the CEO's message and dropped in the CEO's name to demonstrate early on that I had done some research, which was well received.

- Company news
This is always a good topic to touch on as an icebreaker. You may well read that the organisation has won an award, acquired a major brand, or reported record profits. You can slip this in to start a conversation. Get this on your mind map!

The above are the key points I always map out before any interview but, as with any exercise, many people don't take the time to do this. Trust me, this is an invaluable tip. I have been asked right at the start of an interview, 'So, tell us what you know about our company.' If you have not prepared, then you may as well leave the interview at this point because this signals to the interviewer that you're not interested in the company, no matter how good your CV is.

Feel free to add any other detail you believe is important to your mind map, but do not make it too busy or complicated. Its purpose is to give you simple, clear reminders during the interview.

Once you have completed this exercise, put the mind map with any other documents you will be taking with you to the interview, as you can use it to prompt you. If you can memorise it, that's brilliant, but I would suggest avoiding stressing about your ability to remember. What I have done is simply place it in front of me during the interview to prompt me. It has always given me peace of mind and a confident edge.

Prepare to Be a Star!

Now that you have captured some facts about your hiring company, you have a foundations for the first part of the interview – the opening discussion, intended to warm you up. The following is a key exercise that will sell you into the role and help you inspire the hiring manager. If you grasp and prepare what I am about to share with you, then you will significantly increase your chances of being offered the job you desire. You do not necessarily have to draft these out onto paper, but doing so definitely helps.

So what am I guiding you to? It is called the STAR method of responding to certain interview questions – something I was specifically trained in, as an interviewer, to encourage applicants to provide a fully rounded answer to the given question.

The objective of this technique is to respond to a question in a structured manner. I have included, in appendix C, a STAR example for you to consider and learn from.

What I have learned is that if you know your own STARs before an interview, you arrive prepared to give excellent answers to classic interview questions, including 'Can you provide an example of implementing an improvement?'; 'When have you led a team to achieve objectives?'; 'Do you have an example of managing conflict?' There are many such questions, but this should help you get an idea of the classics.

STAR stands for:

S – Situation (background, set the scene)

T – Task or Target (specifics of what was required, when, where, and with whom)

A – Action (what you did, skills you used, behaviours, characteristics)

R – Result (outcome, what happened? e.g., 'I saved the company £100,000')

STAR is all you need to remember to give succinct and powerful answers. Discuss the *situation* you were presented with, the *task* you were given or created, the specific *action* you took, and what the *result* was. Emphasise the result you achieved, as this is a key feature hiring managers look for (e.g., reduced processing time by 30 per cent, saved £100,000 in software costs, reduced cost of inspection by £1 million). Results like this trigger buying signals for hiring managers.

I encourage you to reflect back on your career, if you are not just starting out, and write down three to four key STARs. Get them crystal clear in your mind. I use my CV career highlights, especially those in which I have made savings, and talk about them. If you are just starting out in your career, you may have achievements in your life such as academic awards that can be used to create your unique STARs.

I cannot stress enough how valuable this question-answering technique will be for you. Calling it 'life changing' may sound like an exaggeration, but if you haven't used it, I feel that's an accurate description of what this can do for you. The STAR method will enable you to answer tough work-related questions (not limited to job interviews) in a subtle, compelling, and powerful manner.

People like hearing stories. Facts are easier to remember if they're wrapped in a story. Stories also tend not to get interrupted. Basically, stories are an ancient, proven method of getting a message across. If you tell a story, listeners will remember more of your answers and the messages within them, and you'll deliver your message in a friendly, likeable style. If you use them in a job interview, your chances for success will go off the scale.

The STAR method and stories are two key approaches to creating the right influence during the interview and to demonstrating your proactive attitude and self-knowledge. Knowing your STARs enables you to communicate a clear and confident message, so please avoid skipping this essential pre-interview preparation.

Finally, the following may seem obvious and simple to you, yet I want to emphasise it: perception is everything in the job-hunting game, so your attention to your personal presentation is critical to the visual acceptance of the hiring manager. To this end, ensure all your clothing has been cleaned and pressed the night before to create that crisp and fresh appearance. Groom yourself well on the day of the interview. I always have a fresh haircut, trim my nails the night before, and shave well on the day. Basic stuff, I know, but you would be surprised at the number of people who do not pay attention to themselves and wonder why they were never offered the position.

6 THE INTERVIEW

Valuable Lessons Learned

Almost there! You know what you have to offer. Your CV is excellent; you've made it through the initial selection process. You're polished and shining, ready to sell yourself into a role that you want.

In this next step, realise that you are interviewing the organisations' representatives as much as they are interviewing you. This meeting is about relationships as well as your capability to perform the role on offer. You may be nervous about this meeting, but I can assure you that most people feel some nervousness, so it's perfectly natural. In fact, nervousness can be positive, as it can help you deliver a performance that shines. Just ask any professional actor.

Now, let's step through the interview day in stages and consider some key tips from other successful job hunters.

The Journey to the Interview

Whatever your method of travel, you should know your route and allow plenty of time to arrive early. If you are like most people, your mind may well be predicting what might be said during the interview and imagining of the interview scene. This internal processing is quite normal, but it can elevate your stress level, so relaxation and focus are key. Reflecting on the job specification as you travel and clarifying to yourself how you are the right fit for the role are useful, but for many of us, the key to success is to focus on being yourself, as this will help you to communicate in an authentic manner and not like you've rehearsed a script. Trust yourself.

If you have arrived with plenty of time to spare, perhaps an hour, then seek out refreshments nearby to allow yourself to sit, relax, and breathe.

> **Caution! Take extra care if you are eating or drinking, as a stain on your tie or shirt is highly distracting to an interviewer's perception and spoils your crisp, professional image. This happened to me once, and I spent ten minutes in the gents' frantically washing and drying my shirt before the meeting. And if you do eat, make sure you don't have bits in your teeth!**

> **Tip for Smokers! As an ex-smoker with a twenty-per-day habit, I have sat in my car and smoked myself silly before an interview, totally oblivious to the strong smell that it left on my clothes. To a non-smoking interviewer, smokers stink, and you risk losing an opportunity if you are oblivious as I was. So, avoid smoking at least an hour before your interview, and whatever you do, do not sit in an enclosed space if you must smoke. Get out of your car and remove your jacket.**

On Arrival

From this point forward, every person you meet could be the CEO of the company, so consciously make eye contact with and smile at everyone you meet. With each contact, you will create a perception of you, and it is human nature for people to talk.

Greet the receptionist with a warm and friendly smile. He or she is the face of the company and may make a comment to the hiring manager that could form a positive or negative perception of you for the manager. If the receptionist is particularly positive or helpful, then make a deliberate effort to compliment him or her and engage in some small talk. Ask about the company. Does he or she enjoy working there? Is the staff friendly? Is the company performing well? Building a good rapport with this first contact could well secure you the job, so treat the receptionist well, as this person is one of the most important contacts you can make.

Whilst you are waiting in reception, look around you and assess the professional image the company is presenting to visitors. Read the certificates and awards on the walls. Make a note of anything significant that you can use to open the conversation during your interview. If the company has a corporate magazine on display, then browse through it and pick out any significant company news that might be useful in conversation.

You are looking for any information you can use to generate rapport-building conversation in the short time you have. Remember that the final decision on whom to recruit can simply come down to which candidate the hiring manager felt most comfortable with.

First Contact

This is the moment you are collected from reception by either the HR representative or the actual hiring manager. It is the famous handshake moment. Get on your feet and keep your shaking hand free and ready. Make strong eye contact, smile, be the first to offer a shake, and ensure you make a positive, firm connection. Please – no wet-fish hands!

As the interviewer leads you to the meeting room, ensure you keep pace and take this as an opportunity to make small talk. When you get into the meeting and have been offered a seat, it is time to lay out your stall. In a relaxed fashion, place on the desk the items you need to refer to or would like to present so they are at hand when you need them.

The Interview

Allow the interview to unfold naturally as you settle into your environment. Tune in to your interviewer and listen carefully to the conversation and questions that arise. Give yourself a moment to structure your thoughts and then respond with a structured answer. Do not fill any silence by talking on and on or repeating yourself.

> **Tip! It is okay to pause and gather your thoughts. This is a powerful communication skill.**

Notice the body language of the interviewer, or the main interviewer if there is more than one. Adjust your body language to mirror his or hers in a non-obvious way. Throughout the meeting, match that person each time he or she adjusts to a new position. Subtly copy the interviewer as closely as possible. This is an art form to master, so go gently with this technique. For further mastery, I suggest pursuing neuro-linguistic programming (NLP). To learn more about it, Google 'Salad NLP Jamie Smart'. Jamie Smart was my trainer, and I highly recommend his services.

Often, the hiring manager will be accompanied by an HR representative, so during your feedback to questions throughout the interview, ensure that you consciously make eye contact with all the interviewers, even if one or more is silent. Take the lead by initiating a smile.

The content and flow of interviews can differ greatly from company to company, so I cannot coach you on a standard approach here. I can only tell you to demonstrate an open and honest attitude, and focus on projecting warmth and humility to the interview panel through eye contact and your tone of voice.

The interviewer is not just looking for a match in skills – he or she wants to learn about your ability to inspire others with confidence and to know that you have the intelligence to solve problems, the ability to work with others as a team and to be self-directed, and the attitude to be proactive, approachable, communicative, and capable of articulating a clear message. Finding a match to the job specification is just part of this process.

By communicating authentically during this brief interaction, you will put people at ease about who you are and what you want next in life. Interviewers can sense desperation in an interviewee, so your ability to be relaxed about winning this position is also key. You don't want to be so relaxed that you seem disinterested, but you should avoid putting your entire life on the line for this one opportunity. View each interview as practice for the next; it is an educational journey.

When you have answered all the questions asked and delivered your message to the best of your ability, it is time for the critical moment when the interviewer asks if you have any questions. This moment is a golden opportunity to keep people talking and build further rapport with the hiring manager. Whatever you do, do not say no – unless, of course, you're clearly not interested in working for them, which is also perfectly acceptable and natural.

Assuming you do want to work for them, have two or three key questions prepared for this moment. One I always use is, 'What are the three key characteristics you need from the ideal candidate?' This is a great question that puts the interviewer on the spot while he or she really consider what the company wants from the role. Listen closely to the response and write down some notes. Think about what you have discussed during the interview and how the information you have told the hiring manager matches these three characteristics. If you have not yet covered this in the interviewer, then say now, in a brief overview, how you match these three key characteristics.

This is also a great time to share any achievements, awards, letters from customers, or character references as objective evidence that you are the right person for the role. Interviewers often like being shown objective evidence, as it is something tangible that supports the information you've presented both in your CV and during the meeting.

Tip! If you have brought something with you to show the hiring manager, you do not have to wait until the

end of the interview to present it. Seize any opening that naturally arises to provide evidence that will inspire him or her to hire you.

Keep the interviewer talking as long as you can, but also manage the time well, as other candidates may have appointments after yours. Watch the interviewer's body language and listen for his or her closing comment.

Closing the Meeting

No matter how well you believe the interview has gone, closing as you began is key. Thank everyone for their time, shake hands confidently, maintain eye contact, and say, 'I look forward to hearing from you.'

> **Tip! Ask for the hiring manager's business card, if he or she has not already given it to you, so you can write a thank-you email with any afterthoughts you may have regarding any difficult questions.**

You can now leave the premises knowing that you have been your authentic, true self; communicated your best message; and asked what you needed to ask to develop your feel for the role and the company. Whatever happens next, know that you have done your best and approached this as a professional. It is a learning experience. Always remember that there is no such thing as failure. There's only feedback!

> If I find ten thousand ways something won't work, I
> haven't failed. I am not discouraged, because every
> wrong attempt discarded is often a step forward.
> —*Thomas Edison*

> Never ever quit, as persistence and
> determination are omnipotent.
> —*Author Unknown*

A Note on Presentations

I am not going to cover presentations in detail in this e-book, but I can offer some key points I have learned over the years. If you are asked in advance to deliver a presentation for the interview and you are not an experienced presenter, you may well have a nervous reaction and decide not to pursue the opportunity. Experience has taught me that when this occurs, it is the perfect time to do the opposite of what your nervous system is telling you and face the fear.

Allow two to three days for the presentation topic or question to settle into your subconscious and to come up with ideas of what you might deliver in your talk. As soon as the ideas start flowing, begin the process of creating.

> **Tip! PowerPoint is now the standard platform for presenting, so learn to use it. It is simple to use to create very effective communications. The skill is to keep your slides as simple as possible. Avoid animations. Your slides should be a guide to what you will discuss. Less is always more. Sketch out your ideas of how you want to structure your message on paper first.**
>
> **Then use these rules to deliver an influential talk:**
>
> 1. **Tell them what you're going to tell them.**
>
> 2. **Tell them.**
>
> 3. **Tell them what you have told them.**

At one point in my career, I could not present to others without my whole body shaking, but with practice, I now enjoy this method of communication, so you should view any presentation request as an opportunity to develop your expertise. If you want some one-to-one support and coaching for your presentation, then feel free to email mycoach@inspireahire.com.

Go for it! You can do it!

7 INTO THE FUTURE

Keeping It Alive

Once again, congratulations! Has anyone told you that you are amazing? Let us assume now that you have done everything mentioned so far in this e-book and have successfully gained the job you wanted. Is this the end of our time together? Well, actually, no! Your job-hunting journey has simply been the beginning of really knowing about yourself, what you have to offer, and where you want to go with your working life.

If you have no desire to pursue further opportunities and wish to remain in your new role for the rest of your working life, then I wish you the very best of luck and thank you for purchasing and applying *Inspire a Hire*. I would highly recommend reading a small book called *Who Moved My Cheese?* to open your thinking to the reality of why we do what we do and what motivates us. It is a simple and short read, but a powerful metaphor for personal focus and realisation.

However, the reality is that lifelong jobs are now very rare. Your ability to add value to yourself, to grow and develop your experience and skills by the work you perform, and to maintain an up-to-date CV will assist you in creating some employment security for yourself.

The next skill to learn is keeping you, as a product, alive and fresh in the marketplace. We already touched on this when we discussed networking in chapter 4.

Think Value Added

The famous guru Tom Peters, whom I mentioned earlier, made a clear point to me several years ago: if you are not adding skills or achieving results in a role, then you are not adding any real value to your CV. Essentially, what the heck are you doing there? In the role for which you have just successfully inspired a hire, keep in mind the following key question as you journey on your new path: What am I achieving that will add value to my CV? When you have a clear idea of having made an achievement, update your CV, as it is a living document, and do this regularly.

With every new update, revisit your previous job sites and post up-to-date versions of your CV. This has the potential to create opportunities for promotion and financial advancement within a short period of time, and you won't have to wait for people to retire or for new opportunities to emerge at your current employer. The same principle applies to your network of recruiters and professional contacts. Once updates are available, distribute your details to your network to let them know that you have added a new skill or experience to your profile. This may well arrive at a time when there is a need in the market. I have always left my CV live on job sites, as this results in new contacts and approaches which create opportunities for change, promotion, and growth of my network.

> **Tip! Every approach from a contact is important, as it has the potential for future employment opportunities, so always respond with 'thank you for the contact' and explain your current situation and what you hope for in your next role. Save *all* contact information, to build your network.**

Once you have settled into your new role, identify opportunities for specific training and development that take you in the direction you desire, be it personal growth or attention from outside your organisation. The key question to ask yourself is, 'What do I really want?' Then check the evidence you have around you to see if you are getting what you want. This will cultivate a dynamic change process for you and will prevent stagnation.

The message of this chapter, then, is quite simple and brief: add value, not dust, and update your network regularly to keep it all alive. Do these two things to enhance your chances of success. This leads nicely into the final chapter on what success means to you.

8 ▸ DEFINING SUCCESS

The Fisherman and the MBA

I have thought long and hard about the need for this final chapter in *Inspire a Hire* and concluded that arriving at a clear definition of success is essential to personal growth, peace, and happiness. The ideas that follow will be unique and personal to you, as the leader of your life, and this chapter touches on what I call the 'spirituality of success'.

> All human beings desire
> happiness, few seek suffering.
> —*Dalai Lama*

My goal here is to offer you a viewpoint to consider as you make your way in the world of work, career, and life. So I will begin with a short story about the fisherman and the MBA:

> A boat docked in a tiny Mexican village. An American tourist complimented a Mexican fisherman on the quality of his fish and asked how long it took him to catch them.
>
> 'Not very long,' answered the Mexican.
>
> 'But then, why didn't you stay out longer and catch more fish?' asked the American.

The Mexican explained that his small catch was sufficient to meet his needs and those of his family.

The American asked, 'What do you do with all your time?'

'I sleep late, fish a little, play with my children, and take a siesta with my wife. In the evenings, I go into the village to see my friends, have a few drinks, play the guitar, and sing a few songs. I have a full life.'

The American said, 'I have an MBA from Harvard and I can help you! You should start by fishing longer every day. You can then sell the extra fish you catch. With the extra revenue, you can buy a bigger boat. With the extra money the larger boat will bring in, you can buy a second one, and a third one, and so on, until you have an entire fleet. Instead of selling your fish to a middleman, you can negotiate directly with the processing plants and maybe even open your own plant. You can then leave this little village and move to Mexico City, Los Angeles, or even New York City! From there you can direct your huge enterprise.'

'How long would that take?' asked the Mexican.

'Twenty, perhaps twenty-five years,' replied the American.

'And after that?'

'Afterwards? That's when it gets really interesting,' answered the American, laughing. 'When your business gets really big, you can start selling stock and make millions!'

'Millions? Really? And after that?'

'After that – and this is the best part – you'll be able to retire, live in a tiny village near the coast, sleep late, catch a few fish, take a siesta, and spend your evenings drinking and enjoying your friends!'

The fisherman looked closely at the MBA, smiled serenely, and softly said, 'These MBAs, difficult, are they?'

This is an interesting parable. This simple story has shaped what I really want for the remainder of my life as a father. I am not yet a multimillionaire and may never achieve that level of financial success. Does that mean I am a failure? For me, success is about achieving inner peace and contentment, no matter what my bank balance states. I want to enjoy the greater choice that financial abundance affords, but I will not allow money to be a false idol or my reason for being. If I am to be blessed with financial abundance, then I believe the universe will inspire me with ideas and opportunities to create it.

Many people blessed with fame or wealth live in a state of anxiety, depression, and fear of losing all their material possessions. The media thrives on their suffering. I have learned to feel gratitude for the simple things in life that enrich my soul, and I continue to focus on that. In the Bible, Philippians 4:12 sums up this mental state:

> **I know what it is to be in need, and I know what it is to have plenty. I have learned the secret of being content in any and every situation, whether well fed or hungry, whether living in plenty or in want.**

You can regularly have the best caviar and champagne in the world and live in a stately mansion, but if you do not have peace within yourself and exist in perpetual unhappiness, then what have you really achieved?

I feel deeply privileged to have eaten fish and chips on a windy beach with the one I love, cooked over an open campfire, toasted marshmallows with friends and family, to have had picnics in the garden with my daughter, and to have enjoyed many other simple memories that have nourished me more deeply than any amount of money. It has taken me many years to see how blessed I have been and, God willing, will continue to be.

My motivation in writing *Inspire a Hire* is that it will help you and many others achieve a means of generating an income that you will be happy with. The starting point is for you to get clarity on what it is that you want, and then you can take the first step towards obtaining it.

> Every act you have ever performed since the day you were
> born was performed because you wanted something.
> —*Andrew Carnegie*

My final offering to you is the 'Don't Quit Poem' by an unknown author that has fuelled my persistence and determination through many personal challenges in both life and the job-hunting process. For copyright reasons, I cannot include the poem to close off this book, but during your journey ahead, I encourage you to read the poem at http://www.thedontquitpoem.com/thePoem.htm and use it as a source of wisdom and courage on your ongoing journey. May you also find it helpful.

Thank you for our time together.

Good luck, and may you be blessed with whatever you decide is success.

Your Coach,
Rich

mycoach@inspireahire.com

WINNING CV EXAMPLES: THE END RESULT

Stan Woodman, BSc, FMM

21 Rosemary Close, Allenton, Derbyshire DE24 8QL
(Home) 01273 462366 (Mobile) 07718 917735 (Email) stan.woodman@hotmail.co.uk

Quality Profile

A highly qualified quality professional with more than fifteen years' experience from quality technician to quality manager. The foundation of this professional's career is with the high-precision/high-quality British aerospace arena, gaining management experience with Massey Ferguson and then winning the prestigious Fellowship of Manufacturing Management Award as a change agent with Cranfield University. Moving then into the automotive market for MG Rover, he focused on problem resolution and preventative containment action.

Studying part-time, this enthusiastic professional gained an ONC/HNC and BSc in manufacturing with a primary focus in quality and quality systems. As a result of the combined experiential training and knowledge acquisition, this individual has a hands-on approach to personnel management and provides a supportive environment for improvement through knowledge sharing, synergy creation, and individual development. A positive envoy of change, he minimises resistance through the use of effective communication skills, working with colleagues to build open, honest, and productive relationships. *Now, at forty, this experienced professional within GE wants to hone his leadership experience in a first-time Quality Director role.*

Quality Career Highlights

✓ Generated savings of £1 million for Massey as a result of developing an expert understanding of the warehouse management system and eliminating unnecessary inspection.

✓ Served as project manager of a systems project to deliver a bolt-on to SAP solution for the handling of non-conformance materials, resulting in £100,000 savings for Caterpillar.

✓ Designed and developed a database for complaints management and improved the departmental corrective-action processes.

Quality Career Experience

Customer Quality Manager GE Aviation (Aerospace)   **May 2011 to Present**

- Serving as primary interface between the SCU and the customer for resolving customer quality concerns.

- Working with the supplier quality teams to ensure effective 8D resolution and progression of supplier improvement activities.

- Driving response times down to improve customer service.

- Developing the customer relationship and displaying a commitment to regular feedback and quality of communication.

- Presenting to key customer senior executives on quality concerns and supplier-improvement activities.

Quality Engineer Convertus (Aerospace)   **Aug. 2010 to May 2011**

- Investigated non-conformance reports to arrive at 100% corrective action.

- Developed a PFMEA and control plan for the line as the lead engineer for the team.

- Implemented effective quality controls and control plans on the assembly line.

Quality Manager Quantum Elastomers (Aerospace)   **March 2010 to June 2010**

- Handled all customer complaint resolution.

- Conducted internal audit.

- Managed the inspection team (two people).

- Upheld company approvals.

- Managed despatch/trim/inspection (three people).

Continuous Improvement Manager Derby City Council   **April 2009 to Feb. 2010**

- Saved £120,000 by reduced headcount through process improvement.

- Drove continuous improvement/lean throughout the shared service centre.

- Successfully reduced the number of outstanding contracts from 200+ to 60 in the last two months.

- Introduced new working practice and established a focused team.

Quality Engineer Timken   **Aug. 2007 to March 2009**

Quality Engineer Plastique   **Oct. 2005 to Aug. 2007**

Supplier Quality Engineer MG Rover   **Aug. 2001 to Oct. 2005**

Quality Training & Qualifications

1994 BSc in Industrial (Quality) Systems Technology
1991 HNC in Production Engineering
1989 ONC in Mechanical and Production Engineering
2006 Internal QMS ISO9001 Auditor
2003 Six Sigma Green Belt
2007 A1 NVQ Assessor
2008 LRQA Lead Auditor ISO 9001:2000
1990 NVQ Level IV Quality Technician Engineer
2003 Targeted Selection Interviewer
1999 LEAN Trainer Training
1996 IMS Interpersonal Management Course

Skills Summary

- ✓ World-class quality implementation and continuous improvement methods
- ✓ Very knowledgeable on Jurans Quality Tools
- ✓ Excellent interpersonal, group, and presentation skills at all organisation levels
- ✓ Team leadership, formation, motivation, and management
- ✓ Resource recruitment, selection, and training
- ✓ Change management including resolution of resistance issues
- ✓ Strategic business development starting with process mapping
- ✓ Project management from definition to completion and delivery of objectives
- ✓ SAP system requirements; global Kaizen quality tools

Personal

Status: Married.
Dependants: One.
Location: Willing to travel up to 35 miles.

Steve McMulkin

Address: *41 St Johns Rd, Middlewich, Northamptonshire, NE24 2QB*
Mobile: 07954 213475 **Email:** steve.mcmulkin@gmail.com

Leadership Profile

A highly experienced, action-orientated operations and quality professional with ten years' operational exposure and twenty years' experience within the automotive quality arena. Qualified in the development, introduction, and application of all aspects of quality management, with a diploma in business management, supported by MBA study due for completion in Sept. 2013. Decisive, proactive, and commercially aware manager who responds well to pressure and responsibility. Experience has proven that key strengths are managing people and building relationships, demonstrated by the ability to achieve results through others. Currently pursuing senior management/executive operations roles within either automotive or aerospace that will enable me to demonstrate strategic-level leadership skills.

Key Achievement Highlights

- ✓ Saved £130,000 in operational costs by reducing planned labour, goods, and services.

- ✓ Reduced customer concerns 25% year on year and UK customer PPM.

- ✓ Reduced £172,000 in operational costs as a joint objective with the engineering manager.

- ✓ Implemented and maintained TS16949: 2009 Quality System at two separate companies.

- ✓ Designed and developed a new supplier strategy and measurement system during 2004.

Operations and Quality Career Summary

Quality and Systems Manager (Automotive) Avon Engineered Rubber (AER)
(Oct. 09–June 11)

AER were a supplier to ITW, my former employer. AER's managing director, when hearing of my pending redundancy, approached me and asked if I would join them as their quality and systems manager. AER manufacture foam, rubber, and moulded components predominantly for the automotive sector.

- • Managed a team of five and led a full system audit based on the TS16949 requirements and achieved TS16949 accreditation on 6 July 2010 (and ISO14001 certification in March 2011).

- Developed a new process-based quality manual including the seven mandatory procedures.

- Introduced a business operating system for all key performance indicators including internal and customer PPM, internal scrap costs, customer concerns, and premium freight costs.

- Compiled an employee communication presentation that I have delivered to the workforce (98 people on site).

- Developed a new product introduction process that covers all of the APQP elements and PPAP requirements.

- Restructured the quality department to ensure that the current growth was adequately resourced.

- Managed the health and safety systems for the Stafford site.

Various Leadership Roles (13 years) Illinois Tool Works (ITW) (Automotive)
(1996–2009)

ITW Group Quality/Operations Manager	(2007–2009)
ITW Group Quality Manager	(2002–2007)
ITW Operations Manager	(1998–2002)
ITW Quality Manager	(1996–1998)

Summary of Achievements/Responsibilities at ITW:

- Saved £130,000 during 2008 by reducing the labour, goods, and services against plan.

- Managed varying resource levels up to 44 people when operations manager.

- Achieved 70% reduction in customer concerns from an average of 60 to an average of 18 from 2005 to 2009.

- Achieved UK PPM 10 (target <15).

- Achieved 60% improvement in supplier-related issues during 2007, 25% during 2008.

- Introduced 5s audit system to achieve an improved standard during 2008.

- Completed a managing finance course and contributed to annual and long-term finance plan.

- Achieved £76,000 inflationary cost recovery to offset material price increases.

- Achieved £172,000 in cost savings through reduced material sizes, material specification changes, reorganising of the assembly cell layout, review of shipping administration.

- Reduced defects from 75 to 15 parts per million (PPM) in 2004.
- Reduced total quality costs by 51% in 2004.
- Designed and developed a new supplier strategy and measurement system.
- Achieved 100% on-time delivery (eliminated late deliveries).
- Reduced tool changeovers reduced from 6 hours to 4 hours.
- Successfully implemented ISO 9000, Q1, VDA6.2, and ISO 14001 within 6 months.

Previous Positions

Quality Manager – Martin & Field Ltd	1992–1996
Senior Quality Engineer – Adkins Engineering	1989–1992
Quality Engineer – Precise	1987–1989
All-round Quality Inspector – Turnbulls	1986–1987
Quality Engineer – Gills Cables Ltd	1981–1986

Qualifications/Skills/Training

- HNC – Mechanical and Production Engineering
- MIQA – Quality Management – A3 Quality Assurance management exam
- CIIM – Certificate in the Institute of Industrial Management
- CBA – Certificate in Business Administration
- Managing Finance – Open University
- IOSH Managing Safely
- NEBOSH national certificate (health and safety)
- Six Sigma Green Belt trained at Jaguar/Land Rover

Personal

I am passionate about football and I am a level 1 Football Association coach, managing players under 11. I also enjoy climbing, walking, wildlife, and golf.

Alison Jones

Rose Cottage, Aldridge Lane, Switherstone, Leicester, LE10 8JD
(Mobile) 07825 384672 **(Home)** 01455 619230 **(Email)** ajones@gmail.com

Personal Profile

A focused individual who achieves and exceeds goals, as demonstrated at Hawsworth Community College, where I was awarded Hawsworth Hero. Currently looking for a full-time job where I can add value with my knowledge and skills, develop my capabilities for the future, gain new experiences after finishing my education.

Over the past year, I have expressed my creativity and determination in many different ways, including photography, fashion, and hiking. I have worked independently with an entre-preneurial spirit, successfully running a small online business selling vintage clothing. My excellent skills in ICT have enabled me to set up my business by researching the market and by creating financial spreadsheets of sales, a page to sell my items, and a logo. Taking pride in this small business, I have achieved 100% positive feedback from buyers. My long-term career goal is to be a teacher and to provide a service to people in some positive way.

Key Skills Summary

- Excellent interpersonal skills

- Customer-service orientated

- Capable of learning new techniques quickly and bringing new ideas to the workplace

- A confident worker

- Ability to build a rapport with people of different cultural backgrounds and ages

- A can-do approach to work

- Dependable with excellent communication and timekeeping skills

- Good at problem solving and thinking on my feet

- Focused on having and implementing a plan

- Adaptive to different working environments

- Mature and responsible individual

- Work well using my own initiative or as part of a team

Work Experience

Sales Assistant Dorothy Perkins   (Nov. 2011–Present)

Whilst working part-time for Dorothy Perkins, part of the Arcadia Group, I have had excellent customer feedback to my managers and have had many different duties, as follows:

- Checking tags and pockets
- Opening accounts
- Running the till
- Dealing with customers
- Maintaining the stock room, shoes, and changing rooms

Bar Tender/Waitress Blue Pig Pub   (Nov. 2011–May 2012)

To achieve additional income, I took up bartending at my local pub, getting to know the locals and how to serve and pour drinks depending on customers' needs. I worked busy shifts such as Christmas Eve, Christmas Day, Saturday nights, and a few Sundays, sometimes even managing the restaurant on my own, making sure that everything ran smoothly. This experience gave me increased confidence in dealing with customers and a new skill.

Assistant Caterer Eleanor's Pantry – Temporary   (June 2011)

Worked with Eleanor's pantry, an outdoor catering business. I gained experience in the van, making sandwiches for breakfast and lunch for the customers, and after a few shifts doing this, I went for the weekend to help with a popular dog show, serving the judges breakfast, lunch, and dinner. My duties here were:

- Maintaining excellent service
- Preparing food and the dining area
- Serving the customers
- Making sure cooking areas were clean and organised

Volunteer Age Concern   (2011)

At Age Concern, I gained experience in retail and helping charities. My duties here were:

- Pricing up stock
- Steaming stock
- Working the shop floor
- Operating the till

- Dealing with customers
- Maintaining the stock room

Bar Tender/Waitress Bricklayers Arms (2009–2010)

During my employment with the Bricklayers Arms, I developed a strong understanding of health and safety standards in catering, of team work, and of how to work under pressure.

My duties were:

- Preparing various foods
- Assisting the chef
- Waitressing
- Checking the kitchen, including the fridges

I also have experience working in hostels, with children, with the mentally ill, and with the homeless assisting my mum as she ran art classes, food classes, and many other exciting activities for them. I would go along once a week to these classes, gaining knowledge and experience working with different individuals. I found this experience enlightening, as it opened up my eyes to new things. I knew from then that helping others was something I really wanted to do.

Education/ Qualifications

Hawsworth Community College (2008–Present)

Hawsworth High School (2005–2008)

AS Level Grades: Media Studies (A), Sociology – Education and Research Methods (B), Sociology – Family (C), Information Communication Technology (D)

A2 Predicted Grades: Media Studies (A), Sociology (B), Information Communication Technology (C)

GCSE: English Language (C), Media Studies (A), Information Communication Technology (C), Information Technology (A), Textiles (C), English Literature (D), Maths (D), Improving Your Own Learning (B), Science (Double B), ALAN English (B), ALAN Maths (B)

Interests

Fashion, travelling, adventure, climbing and trekking up mountains. Experiencing different cultures, food, languages, and music. Conducting promotional work with local bands, consisting of organising gigs, selling merchandise, and managing start-up bands. This last interest has given me lots of experience throughout the music scene, enabling me to really think on my feet.

Russell Kendell

5 Angel Close, Penrin, Worcestershire WC17 8GF

(Home) 02526 675188 (Mobile) 07321 456875 (Email) kendellruss@google.com

Professional Profile

A highly motivated and positive professional with twenty-six years' experience in various careers, the most recent being in the building industry. Having had an interest in property development for the last thirteen years, I successfully built an international property portfolio alongside regular employment. In the last eight years, I was directly involved in six substantial building projects from conception to completion. This has included timber-frame housing comprising eight apartments on a two-level build and fourteen apartments on a three-level build.

Experienced also in financial services, retail management, and social work, which have all helped me develop valuable skills in leadership and management of people, organisation and deployment, as a liaison with outside statutory bodies, as a builder of excellent and reputable relations, in negotiations and sales, in time management and the ability to work under pressure for quantifiable results, and in report writing and public speaking in court.

As a positive envoy of change, minimising resistance through the use of effective communication skills, I am used to working well with colleagues to build open, honest relationships in a pressured environment for the good of the company.

Career Highlights

- ✓ Building up a personal portfolio of property valued at £4.2 million in six years.
- ✓ Generating over £1 million of business from identifying and securing potential clients and creating and maintaining their financial portfolios.
- ✓ Designing and managing all aspects of building construction projects, including quality, controlling of costs, time management, management of construction workers, and liaising with suppliers and statutory bodies.
- ✓ Providing rehabilitation and a supportive learning environment for improvement and change, in conjunction with outside statutory bodies, for families at risk in the community.
- ✓ Identifying and implementing changes for retail establishments not earning profits and turning them into efficient, profitable organisations.

Career Summary

Director/Owner RTK Property Management   (2009–Present)

- Identifying and obtaining all aspects of internal and external building work and managing projects through to completion.

- Attending housing exhibitions to aid in the selling of building products for Leica Geosystems.

Director/Project Manager Kensire Homes Ltd   (2004–2009)

- Director and project manager of three traditional builds.

- Raised finance.

- Liaised with architects, building merchants, and building contractors.

- Developed good supplier relationships.

Financial Director Kepp Ltd   (2002–2004)

- Raised finance, controlled costs, and maintained generally oversight of three timber-frame builds.

Independent Financial Consultant Self-Employed   (1997–2007)

- Generated and nurtured leads by networking through solicitors, estate agents, accountants, and personal recommendations to build and maintain a substantial client portfolio with very successful results.

Assistant Manager Coventry & East Mercia Coop Retail Management   (1990–1995)

- Starting initially as a trainee manager, progressing to assistant manager in the larger outlets and then to manager of various stores. Was placed in low-performance stores to identify areas of vast leakage and to implement techniques to aid performance and establish a focused team of workers, changing the store into a successful profit-making establishment.

Residential Family Worker Social Work   (1987–1990)

- Aided the rehabilitation and education of families who had abused their children and observed the possibilities for their being nurtured back into the community with the liaison of other statutory bodies. As a team leader, I was responsible for daily assessments and working closely with the families, daily staff information meetings, writing case reports and reports for court, as well as court representation and liaisons with police, senior social workers, NSPCC, solicitors, and courts.

Training and Qualifications

2004 NHBC course and registration

2002 Mortgage qualification financial services

2000 Diploma in financial planning – certificates 1, 2, 3

1995 Licensee certification course for retail management

1991 Communication and development course with social services

1986 A levels, sixth form college

1985 AS, sixth form college

1984 O levels/CSE, Bluecoats School

Key Skills Summary

✓ Excellent interpersonal and group communication skills with outstanding perception at all organisational levels.

✓ Strong ability to generate business opportunities and achieve targets. Excel in meeting deadlines and exceeding targets in high-pressure environments.

✓ Team leadership, formation, skill deployment, motivation, and management.

✓ Strategic business-development planning.

✓ Strong project management from conception to completion and delivery on all objectives.

✓ A proven track record in financial services with the ability to nurture potential sales from networking leads to fruition.

✓ High capability to build good customer relationships leading to future recommendations.

✓ A positive, self-motivated, and enthusiastic attitude; seeking continuous self-improvement.

✓ Experienced in writing reports for companies and outside statutory bodies and Reason Why letters in conjunction with KPIs.

Personal Status

Married with five children (2–18 years).

KEY SKILLS SUMMARY: VERY USEFUL LIST OF KEY SKILLS

Organisation, management, and leadership: The ability to supervise, direct, and guide individuals and groups in the completion of tasks and fulfilment of goals.

- ✓ Initiating new ideas
- ✓ Handling details
- ✓ Coordinating tasks
- ✓ Delegating responsibility
- ✓ Teaching
- ✓ Coaching
- ✓ Counselling
- ✓ Promoting change
- ✓ Selling ideas or products
- ✓ Decision-making with others
- ✓ Managing conflict

Communication: The skilful expression, transmission, and interpretation of knowledge and ideas.

- ✓ Speaking effectively
- ✓ Writing concisely
- ✓ Listening attentively

- ✓ Expressing ideas
- ✓ Facilitating group discussion
- ✓ Providing appropriate feedback
- ✓ Negotiating
- ✓ Perceiving non-verbal messages
- ✓ Persuading
- ✓ Reporting information
- ✓ Describing feelings
- ✓ Interviewing
- ✓ Editing

Human relations: The use of interpersonal skills for resolving conflict and relating to and helping people.

- ✓ Developing rapport and trust with teams
- ✓ Being sensitive
- ✓ Listening
- ✓ Conveying feelings
- ✓ Providing support for others
- ✓ Motivating
- ✓ Sharing credit
- ✓ Counselling
- ✓ Cooperating
- ✓ Delegating with respect
- ✓ Representing others
- ✓ Perceiving feelings
- ✓ Being assertive

Research and planning: The search for specific knowledge and the ability to conceptualise future needs and solutions for meeting those needs.

- ✓ Creating ideas
- ✓ Identifying problems
- ✓ Imagining alternatives
- ✓ Identifying resources
- ✓ Gathering information
- ✓ Solving problems
- ✓ Setting goals
- ✓ Extracting important information
- ✓ Defining needs
- ✓ Analysing

Work survival: The day-to-day skills that assist in promoting effective production and work satisfaction.

- ✓ Implementing decisions
- ✓ Cooperating
- ✓ Enforcing policies
- ✓ Managing time
- ✓ Attending to detail

THE STAR EXAMPLE: A POWERFUL TECHNIQUE

A STAR story should be approximately two minutes long and delivered with energy and enthusiasm. It should describe something you are proud to have achieved and should be about a real experience you have had (at work or elsewhere), provided it describes a relevant skill or behaviour. Consider the following as an example:

Question: Have you ever led a team before?

This is a closed question which only requires a yes or no response. However, this question opens the opportunity for you to deliver a prepared STAR to expand on the yes. This is why the STAR method is so valuable. Leadership is an important skill, and you must not miss your chance to shine. A lot of folks would give the easy answer here. You, however, have a great chance to impress the audience and make their job easy.

The following is a STAR example response to the above question:

Situation:

Yes, in my last company where I was a software developer. The situation was that a critical project, which had lots of sales and marketing investment riding on the product launch, fell behind schedule when the team leader became ill and had to leave.

Task:

My task was to assume total leadership responsibility for the completion of the product coding and deliver a finished product in line with the latest launch plan.

Action:

Having been a sports captain at school, I loved the challenge of leadership, so I volunteered for the role. Using my technical analysis skills, I was able to identify errors in the initial coding.

Through negotiation with the product director, I implemented the incentive of a small project-completion bonus and, combined with a budget for a few late-night pizza evenings, I led the team to focus on delivering the product.

Results:

The software was delivered on time, with an improved target fault tolerance, and I was promoted to team leader as a result of preventing costs due to project launch failure.

This answer is fully rounded. It not only answers the leadership question asked, but it also conveys the specific skills and behaviours the interviewer is interested in.

When you come up with your own STAR story, you should practice it out loud with a friend or partner until you are confident and the story flows. Being able to articulate an answer fluently to such a question will make you stand out from the crowd as an influential communicator, which is an essential skill in the world of business. Robert Lawrence's *Killer Interview Secrets* will help to further expand your STAR skills.

CV TYPES: A LITTLE BACKGROUND INFORMATION

Chronological CV

A chronological CV presents your experience with each employer, with the positions listed in reverse chronological order. It also contains education and qualification details together with information on hobbies and interests, if these are included. Some chronological CVs also contain a brief personal statement at the front, which sets out the key skills and strengths of the candidate. This is the most common type of CV.

Advantages

- It is particularly useful for those staying within the same industry, as it will demonstrate your career progression.

- It is the favourite format for most employers, who simply want to get a feel for your career to date.

- If you do not have many achievements across your career, taking a job-by-job approach will save you from creating a separate achievements section (characteristic of functional CVs) which may look tiny.

Disadvantages

- If you have gaps in your employment which you would rather not discuss, a chronological CV will make them more obvious.

- If you are changing careers, a chronological CV will add little information to your new employer, who will be more concerned about the transferable skills that you are bringing rather than the detail of your experience in an unrelated sector.

Functional CV

Unlike a chronological CV, a functional CV places the emphasis on your skills and expertise rather than on the history of your employment to date. For example, you may have had several work experiences in which you gained some management experience, but they are spread across your career. Presenting all management roles together emphasises your specific experience upfront, without recruiters having to work this out for themselves.

A functional CV typically starts with a personal profile which highlights the achievements, skills, and personal qualities that you possess. This is followed by a succession of sections, each relating to a different skill or ability. These should be listed in decreasing order of importance. Instead of focusing on any particular job, you should describe your experience as an overall picture. Since you are not focusing on any particular past employment, this means you can also include any skills or experience gained in unpaid work, hobbies, or education.

Advantages
- If you have changed jobs frequently, if your experience is a mishmash of seemingly unrelated posts, or if you have several career gaps, a functional CV will place the emphasis on what you have to offer from your whole employment history.

- If you are changing industry, a functional CV will help the recruiter focus on your transferable skills.

- If you are a more mature applicant, a functional CV will take the spotlight away from your age. Legally, you should not be discriminated against because of your age but, unfortunately, this does occur.

Disadvantages

- If you do not have much work experience, you may struggle to highlight achievements in a separate section.

- A functional CV will not enable you to highlight a consistent career progression. If you wish to convey career progression, you should use a chronological format.

- To conclude the CV, you should display a list of employers and employment dates, as well as a section on your qualifications.

Combined CV

A combined CV follows both the chronological and functional format, which makes this CV slightly longer than the other types. You can summarise your roles chronologically and then emphasise your functional experience, or the other way around.

Advantages

- Perfect format if you have a strong career progression with many achievements.

- Enables you to sell your strengths as well as your experience.

Disadvantages

- Lengthier than a functional or chronological CV.

- Failing to create an attention-grabbing profile at the start of the CV may result in the whole CV remaining unread.

- Not suitable for those with little experience or achievements.

- Not suitable for those with employment gaps.

COMPANY DETAILS: A MIND MAP TEMPLATE

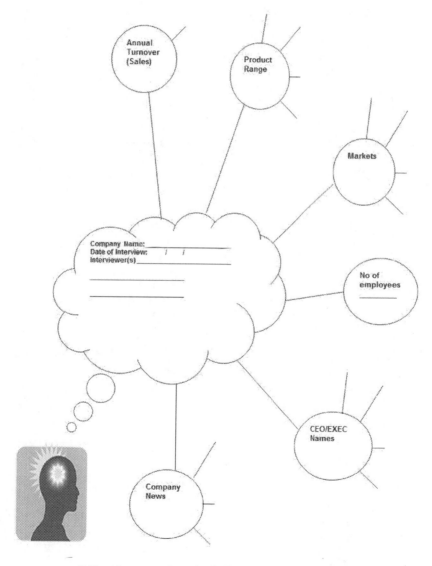

Mind map for job hunter to record

The above are the key facts you need to know about the organisation before your interview. Complete and print the mind map and take it with you to the interview as a quick visual reference.

ABOUT THE AUTHOR

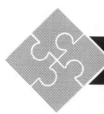

Richard Hobbs commenced his career as a technician apprentice for British Aerospace and graduated, after part-time study, with a bachelor of science degree in industrial systems technology. Now, he is a change agent, certified in 2001 with the prestigious Fellowship of Manufacturing Management (FMM) award at Cranfield University.

He has worked in manufacturing within the United Kingdom, primarily in the field of quality, since 1986, and continues to work in quality management consultancy within industry. As a master practitioner of neuro-linguistic programming, Richard enjoys coaching people to achieve their life and career goals. He welcomes all feedback on Inspire a Hire and offers one-to-one coaching to support the material outlined in this book. Feel free to contact Richard at mycoach@inspireahire.com.